THE STOLEN DECEMBER

Curtis Bobbitt Jr.

Please visit our page to support suicide awareness.

http://www.forevermyasia.com

ACKNOWLEDGEMENTS

I would like to thank, my mother Anita Williams-
wright, my father Curtis Bobbitt Sr., Roger (Catrina)
Inge, Grandmother Patricia Williams, Carolyn
Gilbert, grandfathers Johnny (Jean) Johnson and Rex
Gilbert. My sisters Lexus, Kai, Santremice, Carissa,
Kaylynn, Caz, and Asia Bobbitt. My brothers
Santonis, Joshua, and Kayden. Kyrah Hunter, Ms.
Wanda Stevens, Rahmil Frasier, A K, and Tate.
Special thanks to Aaron Andrews from Torchlight
Academy.
To all my Uncles, Aunts, Family, and Friends: We
love and thank you.

IN MEMORY

This book is dedicated to my sister

Asia Sade Bobbitt

5

NOTE FROM THE PUBLISHER

I met Curtis the same day his mother and I met for coffee to discuss the possibility of publishing his book. If I was already in awe of Anita's strength as I listened to the heartbreaking story of her loss, I was literally knocked off my feet when Curtis came strolling through the door and joined us. Here, across the table from me, sat a kid who had navigated the pits of hell and had emerged to the surface once again – bruised but whole. Reading his words brought me close to tears on several occasions, and there were moments when I wondered how anyone could survive such a pain and go on to live a life of purpose. And then it hit me…through love and faith one can heal all. Curtis and his mother found comfort and healing in their love for each other, and through family and God's love they began their ascent back to living. *The Stolen December* is a document of resilience within the human spirit that will steal everyone's heart.

REFLECTIONS…

I sit here, staring at a blank wall. I am so mad…I am mad because I can't bring back a person I love. I hear my family calling my name, I hear my family and friends telling me they love me, but I cannot feel anything aside from sadness and anger.

I want to go back to the days when my family and I were happy. My mind races against the clock to recapture moments of peace, but I just can't do it. My spirit won't let me. I feel like I have been robbed. I ache at the thought that my family and friends were robbed of the one person we all loved.

God, if you can hear me, I want to call the police and file a report. But tell me, God, if I file a police report what will I say? *Hello, police…I wish to report that my December was stolen forever.*

CHAPTER ONE

When You Were Here With Me (11/30/2015)

I believe this was the best birthday of my life. Why, you wonder? Since you asked, I will tell you: On this day, November 30 2015, my sister Asia and I went to watch the final trilogy of the Hunger Games.

I must thank my older sister Kaí for this amazing memory, because she gave my mother money to take us out for my birthday.

My family and I are close. We look out for one another, and we would give our last dime and breath for each other. I love my sister, and I would have gladly given her my last everything. My sister was the Mockingjay in many senses. I was able to go to her and talk to her about anything.

That night, my mom, Asia, and I stopped at the Cheese Cake Factory to eat. Our next stop was the Regal Brier Creek Stadium where we watched the final installment of the Hunger Games Trilogy.

What unfolded in in the theatre lobby was quite surreal.
My sister and I hugged each another, and. I can't
describe the feeling…it was like embracing an angel. I
remember just looking at her and thinking to myself how
lucky I was.

Asia and I were taking pictures. It was like we were on this runway of *life*. Imagine...another brother and sister celebrities. It was amazing because we were having so much fun. My mom interrupted us and told us she was about to get in the pictures.

Asia and I just busted out laughing because mom was so serious, and I remember my mom trying to look like her feelings were hurt, but she couldn't help laughing. I guess Asia and I had that effect on people. We had so much fun together, that other people wanted to join in. Fun. When I think back, the fun moments of the past are the bittersweet memories of today. I am so grateful for those moments with my sister, and I am so angry because she is not here with me to reminisce about them. I have been robbed of my fun in life, and I have been robbed of my confidant.

I don't know how to move forward. I sit here staring at this blank wall, this frigging wall that has no life or hope. If I hit it hard enough, will I bring my sister back? If I kick hard enough, can I go back in time to prevent her from leaving? To my despair, the answer is no to both questions and I feel hopeless and powerless.

I am so mad…I am mad that I can't bring back a person I love. I hear my family calling me but I shut them out, and sometimes, I wish they would stop calling my name. In some ways, I do not even hear, because a part of me is with my sister. I hear everyone telling me they love me, and a part of me loves them back but the other part belongs to this huge wall of no hope. I just cannot feel anything but sadness and anger.

It is ironic that we went to watch the *Hunger Games Mockingjay Part 2*. I can hardly speak - just like Katniss Everdeen. Grief and pain have their hands around my neck. They are choking the life out me and I can't catch my breath.

I wonder if there is anything I could have done. I wonder if there is something my family should have done. I allow myself to indulge in a blaming game, and maybe it is the only thing that keeps me going.

I wonder if somebody did something to her, and as questions assault my mind, I feel my heart racing.

I cannot eat. I do not want to sleep. I just want to see my sister again. I want what was stolen from me. I want back my December.

CHAPTER TWO

The Game of Trouble

Roger's House

My sister Asia and I would love to go over Roger's house. He was in our lives since I could remember. Roger was like a surrogate dad to me and my siblings, although we knew he wasn't our father. Our real dad was working hard in another state.

Roger and his wife Catrina were a huge part of our lives. I remember my sister dressing up as Minnie Mouse for Roger's daughter's first birthday. Asia left college just to come over and dress up as Minnie Mouse. Kaylynn was so happy!

My sister would do anything for anyone. She was so talented. Everyone who knew her loved her. My sister did not have a mean bone in her body, and she was loyal and loving. I think back and laugh at a conversation Asia and I had before she left for college…I asked her what three things or people she would miss the most. Asia said, without any hesitation: Our mother, her boyfriend

13

Mac and our grandmother's cooking. Asia and our mom were extremely close.

I miss her so much…sometimes I feel sick from it. We were such a close-knit family, and my sister loved us all. I remember her watching me play basketball at Green Road Park. She would have a loving motherly look on her face, and she made me feel like I was a sports hero.

Asia and I loved going to the Park on Green Road because our Aunt Tay Tay lived on that road. My sister was close to us all. She and my grandmother would wear the same shades of lipstick, and I think it is safe to assume that because of them Maybelline was often sold out of red and orange shades.

When Asia was younger, she came home one day wearing lip gloss. My grandma told her that she was too young for make-up, and she should wait until she got older. Then she asked my sister: "who are you imitating out here with that red lip gloss on?" I laughed because I knew my sister was imitating our Grandma Pat.

When Asia got older, she and my grandmother would both wear orange and red lipstick, and don't even get me started with their nail polishes.

I think back to when we would be at Roger's house and play a game of Trouble. I miss little things like that. Asia was our Utopia. She brought us so much happiness and fun, but now that she isn't here, like the characters in The Hunger Games, we live in Dystopia.

I used to love going to my Aunt Tay Tay's house and playing Trouble at Roger's house. I enjoyed going to the movies. I don't love or enjoy anything anymore. I used to be able to talk to Roger about everything. My mom could fix anything. Nobody can talk or fix this. Nobody can help us. Can you mom? Can you change what happened in December?

CHAPTER THREE

A Mother's Memory

From a Mother's Grieving Heart

Asia was the best child I ever had. I know I have other children here on Earth, and I love all of my babies, but I want my Asia here. If she is not here; I want to be where she is. Asia was and always will be my best child

Asia never gave me any trouble. She never got into any fights and she always mentored her siblings. Even her older siblings looked up to her. She and my son Curtis were always extremely close, and if there was any problem in our family unit, Asia would fix it. If there was a party that needed to be planned, Asia would plan it.

My daughter would write the most beautiful poetry. She used to read to me, and I would think to myself: "this is backward…the mother is supposed to read to the child." God! Please bring my baby back to me! She was so perfect. A week before she passed, I told her that she was perfect. I frightened myself a little bit, and I quickly said: "oh, I take it back, I take it back!" Then I held her tightly and said: "I don't want God to take you away from me!"

God, if I wronged in any way. I am sorry. No one is perfect. I just sit on the edge of my bed and I stare at this blank wall. I am so grieved…my heart is so heavy. I am hurting because I cannot bring back my baby. Listen to me, please, God...take me and bring Asia back. I will go. I hear my family and friends calling my name. I am not going to answer them. I am waiting for my child to be placed in my arms. I am not going to sleep. I am not going to eat. I am not going to love. I am not doing anything until my Asia is here in my arms.

Days become weeks and Asia is still not here. I think back to the days when she was with me and my heart becomes so heavy. My face is hot from tears. Asia was a great person, and she was very pretty, simple, humble, kind, and loving. That is how my daughter lived. Asia was real. She was a loving, caring, and aspiring young woman, and she was every parent's dream child.

When you think of having a child and you think how you would want that child to look, act, and talk, everything

17

you think of, that was my Asia. I'm not just saying that because she's gone, but because it is God-honest truth. She was a cheerleader for practically her whole life. She did gymnastics and she played piano. She loved to write poetry; she finished high school and went to Bennett College. Asia said she wanted to be a "Bennett Belle."

The day that Asia graduated from high school, was the happiest I've ever seen her. She was calling everybody saying, "I can't believe this day is here! I can't believe I made it; I'm about to be a high school graduate." I remember her saying it the whole day — "Mom, I made it!" She was so happy!

CHAPTER FOUR

The Approaching Storm. A mother's perspective

I remember bragging about Asia never giving me trouble. Asia had such a genuine patience, and the two of us would talk about anything. Out of all the conversations I had with my daughter, one exchange made me uneasy.

Asia told me that college isn't what it is cracked up to be. I remember asking her what she meant, and she replied that gang rape is a problem in college campuses. I remember my heart stopping for a moment, then racing. I immediately asked her if someone violated her and she told me no. I remember my heart feeling as though it flat lined.

I keep replaying this conversation in my mind and I pray that if anyone knows anything they will reveal what happened to my daughter. I also had a conversation with her about one of my other children. I wondered if I was too hard on one of my children. I want the best for all my children, and I asked Asia in a separate conversation if I was being too hard on her sister. Asia replied: "Mom you just have to listen."

I wonder now if she meant listening in general. I also wonder if she meant I didn't listen to her. Sometimes, I just sit here staring at this blank wall. I look at this wall as if, one day, it will give me answers.

Suddenly things started changing. Asia wanted to join the Army and she wanted to visit home on the weekends more often. She complained of some things happening in her dorm and, she ultimately began to withdraw more and more each day.

As a mother, I tried fixing the issues. A few days before she passed; Asia became increasingly locked into herself. She became short-tempered. Things that she normally would ignore started bothering her. She became a recluse, a prisoner in her own mind, and she started distancing herself from everyone.

I realize now that isolation and irritability are major signs of depression. I remember feeling frightened and shocked, and I didn't understand what was going on. I no longer knew how to communicate with my perfect little girl. Deep down in my soul, I felt something was going to happen.

CHAPTER FIVE

The Eye of the Storm

Curtis' Perspective

I am still staring at the blank wall. I am mad and apathetic, and I can't jump out of the pool of sadness and anger. I float on the surface and I feel detached from myself.

I can't stop the madness. This big blank wall is ticking me off. This big dead wall is ticking me off! I am going to knock it down!

The pain is almost too intense to bear. The day we found out that my mom and baby sister were in a car accident was the day we found out my sister Asia was gone. When the call came it, it felt surreal. We were told that my sister Asia died from suicide and I was stunned. Somebody tell me these are lies, please. Why are our lives all falling apart? This December is taking everything from me.

God! I haven't asked for anything in a long time, but I am asking now. I just want my sister back. I just want my mother and baby sister to be alright. God! I just want my December back. God, if you don't give me December back, I will call the police!

I will call the police and file a report. *Ring. Ring. Ring.* "Hello. Hello, police, my sister was taken from me. My mother and my baby sister were in a car accident. Everything is going wrong today. I just want this day given back to me. I wish to file a report on my stolen December."

CHAPTER SIX

A Family's Nightmare

Anita's Insight

I was in a car accident about two hours prior to Asia passing. A lady was on her cellphone, and she hit me so hard that my car was totaled. My baby flew out of her car seat, and we both ended up in the hospital.

I remember being in the hospital and separated from my baby. I had a feeling that something was wrong. All of sudden I saw my family walking towards me with a grieved look on their faces. I immediately panicked about the baby. Finally, they told me that my third born was gone. It had to be a nightmare…maybe I was knocked unconscious during the accident and I was dreaming. Or maybe it was a lie…not my Asia Sade! Then I remember being told she died from suicide. Oh no! The devil is a lie! Not my Asia Sade!

I felt like someone kicked me in the stomach. My heart and spirit were ripped away from me, I could not move and I could not speak. I just screamed, and I wished I didn't survive the accident. I bore six babies, not five. I have four little girls, not three. The devil is a lie!

I told my mother, "After we get done burying her, get ready to bury me."

Bury me deep, God. I cannot go on. After we get done burying her, get ready to bury me.

CHAPTER SEVEN

Unanswered Questions

I buried Asia on December 19th, and of course her
insurance policy was not honored because of the cause
of death. I believe that suicide is a result of mental
illness, and as any other illness it should be considered a
medical issue. But Asia was never treated because she
was never diagnosed. My mission now is to raise
awareness to suicide and the importance of mental
health. I must state that my daughter did not commit
suicide. You commit crimes, you commit murder, you
commit adultery, but you die *from* suicide.

Asia died from suicide. She did not commit suicide. We
need to raise awareness and remove the stigmas of
insidious killer. So many people think of mental health
issues as purposeful, and some believe mental health
issues are a sign of weakness, but depression is just like
any other disease.

The devil tries to bring people down. My daughter was
an angel, and the devil knew this, as he wouldn't bother

to attack someone he thought was POWERLESS. The attack level confirms his fear of one's power!

I could have died when my brother died, and I could have died when my daughter died, but I will continue to live until I see them again.

I prayed for my son through the storms, and I look at him as my motivation to go on. Keep pushing and tell your story, ForeverMyPrince.

CHAPTER EIGHT

Putting the Pieces Back Together

Curtis Bobbitt's words to his sister

Every day is a struggle for us. I don't understand what I was going through and I wondered if, maybe, I didn't say the right thing nor did the right thing to keep you here. I would have never left you, Asia. I feel robbed by that day.

I feel like I am going to die too. One day you are here, and the next day you are gone. I could accept it more if you died in a car accident, or if someone took you from us. At least I would have somebody to blame. I would have someone else to blame rather than us.

I no longer eat. I can't swallow food because I feel like I will choke if I do – my throat is closed. I am riding in cars, about to jump out. The world is moving so fast, and mom is taking me back and forth to the hospital.

Doctors say I have anxiety because of your passing. I don't have anxiety…I have animosity! I am mad as hell!

I am mad that you are not here. I am mad because I didn't see the signs! I am angry because I can't take back December.

I sit here, staring at this big blank wall again. I am so mad. I am mad that I can't bring back a person I love. I hear my family still calling my name. I wish they would leave me alone. I am about to punch another hole in this wall.

I hear footsteps running down the hall. My little brother and sister are going to tell our mom on me; for not answering them. Oh man, I hear my mom coming now. There she goes, knocking quietly on my door. If I don't answer her, she is just going to stand at the door calling me. "Curtis? Curtis? Are you okay? Curtis?"

"Come in mom," I said to her. I was ready to tell her to leave me alone, but I couldn't say anything. My mom slowly walked towards me and we both just broke down crying. For the first time since you left, I understand we all are missing you, Asia.

Mom held me and told me, "I had to bury your sister…I'll be damned if I bury you." I can't go with you Asia. I wanted to be with you, and I was trying to leave here by not eating and jumping out of cars. I didn't want to admit it, but I will tell you now… I will always love you, but I can't hurt mom this way.

I am beginning to eat solid foods now. I finally ate a piece of pizza! I went over Mrs. Wanda's house that same day mom and I talked. Mrs. Wanda, her husband, and son were all there. My mind was still a bit fuzzy, but all of a sudden, pizza was delivered, and it reminded me of when you were here. I felt like you were telling me that everything will be alright.

For a moment, Asia, it was like you were here. I scooped up a slice of that pepperoni pizza; Sis, and I ate it! It was so good! Mrs. Wanda started crying and I was going to give her a hug, but the pizza Sis…the pizza was so good! I will always wonder how you are, and I will always feel you around me.

I still look into the sky and wonder how you are doing. When the wind hits me a certain way, I feel you around me. Damn Sis… I miss you. I know I owe it to others to help. I can't sit around wishing to die. I can't waste time being angry. I owe it to you; to live. I owe God everything.

These pieces are heavy, and I am never going to understand. I am never going to agree. One day I will have a little girl named after you. One day I will be able to hold you close. When the wind hits me a certain way, I know you are saying hello to me.

Peace

Anita Williams-wright

Every day is a struggle for me and our family. I will
always say your name in my sleep. You will always be

my baby girl. I will always light a candle for your memory. In our house, we hold your memory. In my heart, I hold your legacy. When I take them walks—I feel you right beside me.

On that day—when The Lord calls me—Asia Sade, I am going to run so fast up Heaven's Stairs. You just save that spot for me.

Peace

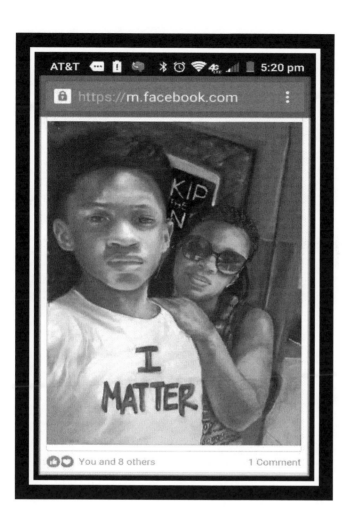

CHAPTER NINE

Forever Our Asia!

If anybody was to ask me whom I blame, I would have to say that I don't blame anybody, but I do feel that there should be more awareness about suicide. So much information about depression and self-harming is kept under lock and key because of social stigmas that if something is not done to reverse this trend, it will keep on growing like a cancer, undetected until it is too late. You can't stop the devil if you don't expose it. God has power, but so do we.

Parents must learn to listen. We think we know everything, and we fool ourselves into complacency. I hear so many parents – and I, too, am guilty of it – telling their kids that since they have no kids, bills, or serious concerns, they really have nothing to be stressed about.

To those parents I would like to say to please listen to their children. I can hear Asia in my ear, telling me to listen. Just listen to your child. Listen to your friend. Listen to your mother. Listen. Just listen. Be that ear.

My daughter did make a plea for help, and no one listened or thought she was serious. The day she passed, she told her friend that she wanted to die, but he dismissed her. I don't blame him. The reason I am bringing this up is to raise awareness. If someone tells you that they don't want to live, or that they want to kill themselves, contact 911 and reach out to their families. I owe my daughter everything that I'm doing. That's why I'm strong. She will be, always and forever my Asia.

It's Ok...

Goodbyes
are not forever,
Goodbyes are not the end,
they simply mean
I'll miss you,
until we meet again.

Say My Name!

Asia

43

44

A FAMILY MOURNS

Tell me it is a dream.

Tell me this wall—leads to another place.

Take,

Take,

Take this pain away.

Take this grief far away from me.

Can we go there, to that distant place?

Can we run up those stairs?

Tell me, so I can bring you back from there.

Take,

Take,

Take this anger away.

Take away this anger and animosity.

What happened?

What went wrong?

Tell me, so I can bring you back right here.

Asia, mommy be calling out your name in her sleep.

Asia, I am fasting to bring you back to me.

Asia, Kaí and the rest are a little less kind.

Asia, when you left; a part of us died.

Asia, thank you for the memories!

We will be hugging and talking it up when we see one
another again!

Poem Donated

Michelle Carter-Douglass

created just for you by: Delbra Jones

48

51

http://www.forevermyasia.com

Made in the USA
Columbia, SC
08 June 2020